Other Books

by Michelle Leclaire O'Neill

Creative Childbirth

Hypnobirthing: The Leclaire Method

Twelve Weeks to Fertility

MEDITATIONS for
pregnancy

For my children,
Brendan, Erin, and Maria,
and my granddaughter, Ava

Suddenly, as if without a reason,
Heart, Brain and Body and Imagination
All gather in tumultuous joy together.

—Harold Munro

MEDITATIONS for PREGNANCY

36 Weekly Practices for Bonding with Your Unborn Baby

Michelle Leclaire O'Neill, Ph.D., R.N.

Andrews McMeel Publishing

Kansas City

The material in this book is intended for education. It is not meant to take the place of treatment by a qualified medical practitioner or therapist. No expressed or implied guarantee as to the effects of the use of the recommendations can be given or liability taken.

04 05 06 07 08 RR2 10 9 8 7 6 5 4 3 2 1

Library of Congress Cataloging-in-Publication Data
O'Neill, Michelle LeClaire.
    Meditations for Pregnancy : 36 weekly practices for bonding with your unborn baby / Michelle LeClaire O'Neill.
        p. cm.
    Includes bibliographical references
    ISBN 0-7407-4711-8
        1. Pregnancy. 2. Meditation. I. Title.

RG525.O43 2004
618.2—dc22

2004055090

Book design by Desiree Mueller

contents

INTRODUCTION
The Experience of Expecting

Within this book, you'll discover simple weekly ways of connecting to your body, your emotions, and your yet-to-be-born baby. These connections will help to create the smartest, safest, most intelligent, and most valuable beginning for your uterine guest and yourself.

The experience of your baby growing inside becomes more available to you when you can feel her moving inside you. The purpose of this book is to help you to enhance this experience by becoming aware. By being aware, you share directly in the union between you and your baby, and you will experience the richness of your pregnancy. This book is not about the concept, the science, or the idea of pregnancy. It is about the loving relationship between you and your baby that begins at conception. You can become aware through your senses and through sensations from this new connection to your unborn baby and from your cellular memory of past connections in the world. You bring to this developing love your awareness of each moment and an awareness of thoughts and emotions that might otherwise remain dark and silent to your mind, thoughts, and emotions. These may affect your perceptions without your even realizing it. Your experience of this pregnancy, of this amazing connection between you and your baby, is not merely the result of your sensation of bodily changes such as your growing abdomen and your omnipresent uterine guest. It issues from all your past perceptions and your present realizations. The kind of prenatal mothering and nurturing that you do and the kind of mother you want to continue to be or become are established by your present relationship with your baby.

This book is about your consenting to accept your present feelings, both physical and emotional, and to change those feelings, thoughts, and perceptions that you feel will not benefit your growth and development as well as the growth of your baby and your evolving interaction. This *umbilical code*, which is what I call it when I work with pregnant women like you, is about the meaning of this relationship for you, your intuitive and concrete connections to your baby, both conscious and unconscious. The true awareness of the umbilical code comes about through your stillness, your mindfulness, your willingness, to feel all that is revealed to you. To fully develop the expression of meaning behind this code you need to take time for reflection of this experience, time to courageously connect spirit to spirit with this new reality in your life, in your body, in your mind, in your heart, and in your soul. The essence of your pregnancy is not your baby growing inside you or your growing belly; it is the umbilical connection, the flow, the unique reality of the two of you as one and as two separate yet equal beings. It is the vital union of love between you.

Only you can choose to participate as fully as possible with the umbilical code. You may keep silent your feelings from the world but there are no secrets between you and your baby. The umbilical code is a wordless yet direct message, a direct line that is easily deciphered by your baby. This connection will frame his perceptions, his emotions, his intellect, his mind, his body, and his spirit. The secret of the umbilical code is that nothing is disregarded by your fetus. Yes, your emotions and the food you eat translate into chemicals that are passed on directly to your baby, who is formed by them and affected by them long after your physical separation at birth.

Pregnancy presents a time of possibility for an amazing transformation for yourself limited only by your lack of desire to participate or by fear. I hope you are able to detach from your past so that you may fully experience the drama of the now of your pregnancy. I hope that you will be able to listen to your bodily sensations and to your emotions. I hope you will give yourself permission to feel them so that you are not limited by them. The umbilical code allows the possibility of your own rebirth. You deserve to become all of who you are, as does your baby.

Through this union of love, all things are possible.

MeDITaTIONS for
Pregnancy

HOW TO USE THIS BOOK AND CD

Choose a time each week to read your meditation; they are numbered by the week of your pregnancy to make it easy to keep track. The purpose of each weekly meditation is to help you understand what is going on in your body and to help you be aware of your baby's presence and of your feelings. The meditations are simple and efficient ways of getting you to be present in the now and in touch with this special time in your life and your baby's life.

After reading the meditation, read the affirmation and suggestions. Make a decision to do at least one of the suggestions each week. It is best to make your goal attainable and measurable, for it is better to make a goal easy and meet it than not to meet it and feel like a failure.

Your participation will enhance your peace of mind, your baby's growth and development, and the peace and serenity of your baby. The bonding between you and your baby will also be improved.

Take time once a week to rest and listen to the CD that is included with this book. It will calm your emotions, help you to carry your healthy baby to full term, and relax your nervous system. It will also prepare you for the relaxation that is imperative for a calm, centered, and safe birth, whether it is natural, induced, medicated, or a C-section.

Have fun, and "begin with the magic"!

SECOND MONTH

WEEK 5

Peach blossoms fallen on running stream pass by;
This is an earthly paradise beneath the sky.

—Li Bai

This week your backbone is forming. Some of your vertebrae are in place, and somehow my body knows how to care for and develop this wonder that you are. I hope that my strength and your strength will give you the emotional support to one day stand up for what you believe.

Your brain is more developed now. You are a living being within me, one who can now sense and feel. My thoughts, I realize, become feelings that I send to you. I must take care of what I think and send you nurturing thoughts. I shall relax as much as I can and send soothing messages to you as you float peacefully within me.

You now have buds for your arms and legs. I visualize them forming and wish them well in their growth. One day I'll kiss your tiny toes and feet; you'll grasp my finger and I'll let you hold on for as long as you want. You're receiving so many wondrous gifts in such a short period of time and I bet you're accepting them with ease.

Like my own miraculous spine, I can be flexible yet strong. I can accept the changes in my body and rejoice in the new life that grows through these changes. Today I ask for the flexibility to allow this miracle.

In the broad daylight
Thou art unseen,
but yet I hear thy shrill delight.

—Percy Bysshe Shelley

This week, I will:

- Take my prenatal vitamins daily to help your growing body and find at least one day to practice a few of my stretching exercises to keep my spine flexible.

- Sip miso soup or ginger or peppermint tea if I'm having nausea or morning sickness to calm my stomach and to provide hydration. (I won't use ginger or ginger tea after the first trimester, however, because it may cause miscarriage.)

To make miso soup, take 1 tablespoon fresh yellow or white miso paste and dissolve in 1 cup boiling water. Drink warm. This is also good to sip throughout labor because it helps maintain proper pH balance in the body. Fresh miso is sold in many supermarkets and most health-food or natural-food stores.

WEEK 6

That's the wise thrush; he sings each song twice over
Lest you should think he never could recapture
That first fine careless rapture.

—Robert Browning

You have two folds of tissue that will grow to be your sweet ears. The magical convolutions of your ears are taking place inside of me. May you hear the sounds of love and equality and peace and serenity and joy. The lenses of your eyes are now appearing and—guess what?— there is a tail apparent at the end of your spinal cord, a remnant that connects us to our primal ancestors. This tail will disappear with time, yet may the spirit of freedom, of swinging from tree to tree or walking with tail erect and proud or wagging with delight, remain with you.

You're getting so many wondrous gifts in such a short period of time and I bet you're accepting them with ease. I wish I could say the same. Sometimes I feel a bit anxious about being a mother. In fact, I'm not sure I have even come to terms with being a daughter yet, or a partner. Maybe I can learn from you and just grow and develop in new ways along with you. Perhaps I need to see through new lenses in my own eyes. Perhaps I ought to look differently at some things.

With my own eyes I can see that change can be good: change from winter to spring, when birds gather twigs for their own babies. And the changes that seem bad, perhaps they will slowly evolve into something else, disappearing like the remnant of the tail we all once had. I can become the mother you deserve, accepting change with grace and ease, and welcoming the new into my life.

Your clear eye is the one absolutely beautiful thing
I want to fill it with color and ducks
The zoo of the new.

—Sylvia Plath

This week, I will:

- Choose vibrantly colored foods to enjoy the vitamins they bring you and me: bright orange carrots, green and red cabbage, purple eggplant, white cauliflower, and bright red beets. They will be a feast for my eyes while they help yours grow!

- Observe my own reactions, trying to accept changes with grace and ease: the roundness of my belly and the extra sleep I need.

KITCHARI RECIPE

This is a healing food for pregnancy and is especially good postpartum. Make this ahead and keep it in the freezer or refrigerator to reheat when you're too tired to cook.

1.5-inch piece of fresh ginger, cut into pieces (fresh ginger can be used up until week 10 of pregnancy and during post-partum; *do not use fresh ginger* during the second and third trimesters of pregnancy)
2 tablespoons unsweetened shredded coconut

1/2 cup chopped fresh cilantro
1/2 cup water
3 tablespoons ghee (clarified butter; can be purchased at
Indian food stores or natural-food stores)
1/2 teaspoon ground turmeric
1/4 teaspoon sea salt, or 1 tablespoon fresh miso paste
(yellow or white miso is best)
1 cup yellow mung dahl (mung dahl can be purchased
at Indian food stores or natural-food stores; mung dahl
nourishes all the tissues of the body and is a healing food;
it detoxifies cells)
1 cup basmati rice
6 cups water

Put ginger, coconut, cilantro, and 1/2 cup water into
blender and liquefy. Heat ghee over medium heat in large
saucepan and add the blended mixture, turmeric, and salt
or miso. Stir to mix well and then add mung dahl, rice,
and 6 cups water. Bring to a boil and boil uncovered for 5
minutes. Cover, but leave lid slightly ajar to allow steam to
escape. Turn heat to simmer and cook for 25 to 30
minutes, until rice and dahl are tender. Makes six servings.

week 7

To see a world in a grain of sand,
And a heaven in a wild flower,
Hold infinity in the palm of your hand,
And eternity in an hour.

—William Blake

You are growing inside me, and by the end of this week you'll be a half-inch long. I'll help you this week in your big stretch by eating well and taking prenatal vitamins. By this week, your heart has started to beat inside your tiny chest. It is now truly yours. Our heart rates are different and yet in many ways I am responsible for the way yours beats, as my rhythm affects your rhythm. To help create a peaceful environment for you, I'll walk mindfully and do some stretches to soothe and calm myself.

Right now, your sweet face is forming. This week it flattens and you get little openings for your nose. I wonder whose nose you will have, and whose would I like you to have. Of course, it doesn't really matter as long as you can inhale and exhale easily through your nasal passages and as long as you can appreciate and differentiate smells. This week, I'm going to have fun smelling all the different spices in the pantry. Maybe I'll even take you to the woods or a garden so I can send you the excitement of other scents. I know the smell I'm looking forward to the most, though: your sweet, new baby scent.

This week you also begin to grow muscle fibers. Maybe you can even make micromovements. How interesting it must be to move a muscle for the first time. What a busy week you're having, and I thought I had a lot to do!

As I breathe through my nose, I think of the miracle of your growth. I realize that each fiber of my being is influencing each fiber of your new body, and I take the time to calm myself to observe what makes me angry or sad or joyous. I can observe my feelings and find positive ways to surround you.

Let even obstetricians fall quiet,
For Chloë is on her latest diet
So rapidly our Chloë passes
From bananas to wheat germ and molasses.
First she will eat but chops and cheese
Next only things that grow in trees.

—Ogden Nash

This week, I will:

- Choose foods to help you grow. I'll eat whole grains, leafy green spinach and kale, arugula or Swiss chard. Maybe I'll even try sea vegetables or explore the scents of fresh herbs as I shop, celebrating your new nose.

- Allow any feelings of mine that arise. If they are upsetting, I will be gentle with myself as I try to observe the feelings and understand them.

week 8

Each cell has a life
There is enough here to please a nation.
—Anne Sexton

Well, you are no longer an embryo. You have now graduated
to a fetus and by the end of this week you'll be all of an inch long.
You still don't look like the final you, but by now you have a
jawline and your facial features are becoming clearer.

Your head is about half your size. May your head continue
to be strong and full, and your thinking be healthy and creative
and adventurous. I hope I can guide you that way, and with such
a good start in life, who is to say what your limits and what your
potential might be?

You are also developing your tooth formation. One by one they align above the smooth skin of your gums. You were once just a gleam in my heart's desire, and now you have tooth buds secreting enamel and dentin. Some months after you are born, they will break through your gums and then you'll have twenty magnificent baby teeth.

Although I can't see you, I can feel the surge of your presence within me. What a wonderful thing you are: bit by bit you're coming together and becoming you. The surge of you fills me and makes my heart sing. Happy growth spurt, little one!

Your arms are now long enough so that you can touch your own face. For now, until I can touch you, feel the growth and grace of your head for me. Your larynx has begun to develop. One day you'll have a voice of your own, but until then, I'll listen with my being to the song of your being within me and that will help calm and center me.

Give to these children new
from the world,
Rest far from men!
—William Butler Yeats

This week, I will:

- Eat foods high in calcium to help you grow strong, even teeth: turnip greens, kale, watercress, and whole grains.

- Eat alone and in silence one day, and I'll chew each bite until it becomes liquid in my mouth, meditating on how this food will travel through me to nourish you.

THIRD MONTH

WEEK 9

Invisible, visible, the world
Does not work without both.

—Rumi

This week, we share our new organ together—our placenta. It produces hormones and nurtures you. How efficient it is, connecting us now, manufacturing the estrogen that helps my uterus develop blood vessels for your present home. The progesterone it produces prevents my uterus from contracting strongly until you've reached full term, until you're ready to come out into the world on your own. It is also our fluid poem, our pathway for communication. We send blood and love back and forth, back and forth.

The milk glands in my breasts are beginning to develop. I can remember when my breasts first began to swell and grow and even before then, when I wanted them so that I could look like a woman instead of a girl. Now I'm a bit ambivalent about their growth. I don't want to look like one big mammary gland, but I want to provide your milk, your nourishment. I close my eyes and I'm a little sad, a bit scared, and rather excited.

For the time being, you're drawing your food through your umbilical cord, your connection to the placenta. I close my eyes and wonder if this flow makes a sound, or a vibration, and if you feel it on its way to you.

My skin is a little softer now and I even look a bit younger. Maybe I'm too young to be a mother, or am I too old, or does age have anything to do with it?

My body is anticipating your arrival in this world and you still have quite a long way to go. The feast is being prepared long ahead of your arrival. Perhaps, in the same way my body knows what to do, and your cells know how to grow, I'll grow more and more naturally into motherhood along with each of your growth spurts. May we both progress smoothly and with grace into our new roles, our new bodies.

Maples swell with sap a-syruping!
Nature is spreading herself today!

—Ogden Nash

This week, I will:

- Periodically spend five minutes contemplating the environment I've created for you. With my hands lightly on my growing belly, I'll breathe in and out slowly, sending you warm messages of love.

- Massage my breasts with sesame oil, ghee, or coconut oil, using the oil on my breasts and around them to soothe discomfort. After you're born, I'll use only ghee. That way, if even a tiny bit remains on my breast, it is safe for your digestive system.

week 10

My two breasts that were fine and as
White as are mushrooms
Are now covered with honey, and fingers of moon
Have rounded them as with the pulp of a fruit.

—Helen Wolfert

Now you are about one and three-quarter inches long—not even two inches, yet so much activity! Hard to believe that I was once that size, carried in my mother's womb, and now I am big enough to carry you. My mother, too, was once that size. Someday, you'll think about it, too, perhaps, if you're a girl. Your uterine home has expanded to the size of an orange. How interesting to have a home that grows with you. Still, you and your house are hidden deep within my pelvis. Enjoy your solitude in your custom home. It can get hectic out here.

My breasts are getting heavier. They are a good reminder of what is going on in my body. Sometimes I forget until I'm getting dressed, or I'm working out, or I move too quickly, and then I realize that I need a lot more support. I really am manufacturing milk. How astounding!

Your ankles have formed. I hope the strong connection they form between your feet and your legs will help you walk, run, and jump with pleasure. May you move lightly through life and may your gait be easy and strong.

Your wrists, too, are formed, and your fingers and toes are clearly visible. Years from now, we'll circle them with ribbons and garlands of flowers, and I'll tell you how I dreamed of your bones, of your five perfect fingers fluttering in sacred exhalations of touch like a silk worm's gentle spinning. May you reach out to the world with great wonder and joy. May you nurture and caress well. May you give freely and receive graciously.

Today I relax a bit as your rate of growth slows down. I stop all outward motion and feel the magnificence of my own breath. Then, I think of you and your new limbs. I open my palms and spread my fingers softly. I cannot embrace your touch or count your toes, but I will. Still, I do not quite realize you.

And I will make thee beds of roses,
And a thousand fragrant posies,
A cup of flowers and a kirtle
Embroidered all with leaves of myrtle.

—Christopher Marlowe

This week, I will:

- Choose a new bra to provide more support and perhaps a bra to wear when walking or working out.

- Hold in my palm an orange, thinking of the size of my womb and your tiny form, growing there.

WEEK 11

Let me believe in the clean faith in the body,
The sweet glowing vigour
And the gestures of unageing love.
—Dylan Thomas

The amount of blood circulating throughout my body has begun to increase. I am filled with the energy of an emerging life force within me, red and glowing. The chambers of your heart are forming. May each one of them know love and understanding, and rapture and harmony. Your liver and spleen have matured and are now producing red blood cells. Radiant with the element of life, they march in honorable procession.

Your lymph nodes and thymus are forming white blood cells. These amazing cells know exactly how to keep you free from all sorts of poisons. Today we are responsive to all the healing emissions from the sun and the sky and the air and the moon and the earth and the stars. Now you have testicles or ovaries. Testicles: a sign of male strength, a witness of virility. Ovaries: the exaltation of fruit in female animals and in plants. I have always had ovaries. Is it possible that I now have testicles within me, too, or do I have a whole new cascade of eggs whirling within my womb?

> Today, I honor my strength and remember my body's healing power. I breathe in oxygen, swelling the blood cells with life. Today, and all the days to come, I send my loving strength through my blood to yours, helping you grow and thrive.

When you begin, begin at the beginning.
Begin with the magic, begin with the sun,
Begin with the grass.

—Helen Wolfert

This week, I will:

- Imagine us as one: a single cord stretched between the heavens and the earth. I'll stretch my arms around my growing belly and hug your growing life and breathe in the fresh oxygen on a morning or evening walk, thinking of how the oxygen goes from my nose to my lungs, then to my blood, and then travels through the umbilical cord to your blood.

- Research childbirth classes and perhaps find other expectant mothers to share ideas and information.

WEEK 12

Sleep, my babe; thy food and raiment,
House and home, thy friends provide;
All without thy care or payment:
All thy wants are well supplied.

—Isaac Watts

Now you are about three inches long. I think of you as a leaf: translucent, illuminated, leaning toward the sun. Like the leaf, you turn to forces I don't understand, to spirit and matter, your internal intelligence. Your tiny body knows how to expel what doesn't belong, and your immune system adjusts to my activities and the foods I eat, harmonizing them and using them as you develop. Your mouth opens to swallow amniotic fluid, and it is absorbed into your bloodstream through your very own digestive tract. You then excrete some of it through your kidneys, taking in what is desired, absorbing what is necessary, and letting go of the rest. You're learning the process of life.

Now your face is well defined, and you can move those muscles. I move my hands across my belly, trying to outline your visage, thinking of your features. Your eyes are fused together while mine are gently closed, thinking of you. What color will you be? The color of me? Are you trying these new movements? Are your eyes squinting now? Are you opening and closing your mouth?

I open and close my mouth, and think of yours, opening and closing, and your eyes, opening and closing. I let my body's own wisdom help me to use what I need, and to let go of the rest. I can let the bad moments wash over me, like fluid, and absorb the good moments into my very pores, like the sun on a warm day.

So far from sweet real things my thoughts had strayed,
I had forgot wide fields and clear broad streams,
The perfect loveliness that God has made,
Wild violets shy and heaven-mounting dreams
And now, unwittingly, you've made me dream
Of violets, and my souls forgotten gleam.

—Alice Dunbar Nelson

This week, I will:

- Gently close my eyes in concentration of you. What will you look like? What will you see?

- Eat plenty of green, leafy vegetables, yellow vegetables, and fruit to enhance your immune system. I'll also take my prenatal vitamins with folic acid and iron.

week 13

From a dark and narrow street
Into a world of love.
A child was born, speak low,
Speak reverent.

—Dora Greenwell

Well, my sweet, we're in this together, you and I. I do hope you like the environment that I've created, both physically and emotionally. I do hope that you are comfortable and content. This week my uterus has risen above my pelvis. The doctor and midwife can feel it on external examination and now we'll be checked at least once a month. It's nice to be taken care of by people who know what's happening to us both.

Of course, I have little daily worries—bills and nourishing you and gaining weight. These might be considered minimum concerns, so I try not to focus on them as problems. I'll try to deal with things as they arise and not let them build up into troubles, because you cannot take a continual assault of anxiety hormones. By dealing with issues as they arise, I try to set your emotional thermostat at a healthy level. I really want to do that for you. What a tremendous responsibility! Is this possible?

Your growth and development have become much more subtle. My behavior, however, needs to be explicit, as you are so fine-tuned to my every move. Smoking can cut your oxygen supply. Alcohol can maim or even kill you. No wild nights for me now, just sweet guitars and abstinence.

Of course, you are also very resilient. Occasionally I do ignore your physical needs. What you need is not unreasonable, but I just find discipline difficult at times. I'll continue to do my best, and we'll support each other—sometimes I'll be able to do for you what I might not be able to do for myself.

When I rub my belly, I sometimes feel a surge of love, and I think you feel my touch, my love through the rubbing. Perhaps by thinking of your needs I can acknowledge my own, and honor them. We both deserve love and attention. I send you love now.

She knew this instant would remain
A sacrament not touched again.

—Robert P. Tristram Coffin

This week, I will:

- Rub my belly and chat with you so you can enjoy a tranquil swim and feel protected and nurtured.

- Respect our needs for nurturance and do something special for myself. What should it be? A massage, a facial, a walk in the park, a book I've waited to read, an extra meditation, a nap?

FOURTH MONTH

WEEK 14

The pattern of the atmosphere is spherical
A bubble is the silence of the sun,
Blown thinner by the very breath of miracle
Around a core of loud confusion.

—Elinor Wylie

Now you have clear patterns of movement. You are beginning to move your limbs, making fists and kicking. Though I can't yet feel those tiny movements, sometimes I think I have vague sensations of you. Soon you'll be communicating to me through your arms and your legs, your hands and your feet, your elbows and your knees, and I will do my best to pay attention. You have also established a resting rhythm. I'm not quite aware of that yet, either. I look forward to understanding your communications.

What is it like to move for the first time? You are stretching and thrusting your tiny arms and legs outward. I bet your motions are as gentle as a cloud floating across the sky.

These periods of movement alternate with periods of quiet, motionless sleep. Like a soft breeze you move inside me and then like a quiet mist you hush and rest deeply. One day, you'll watch your hand move for the first time. I recall once seeing a ring of mountains and a layer of whispering clouds hovering in their center, silently protecting all below. In that stillness there was great peace. I'll think of that when I'm restless, or uncomfortable, and need to find stillness and quiet within. I hope you will always keep a space inside you for that grand silence.

And soon you will rise up again, little tai chi movements, wondrous thrusts and stirrings, and I still am unable to really feel that it is you. I admit I am impatient.

I'm waiting in anticipation for a definite movement, some awareness of you. I await your touch.

I offer thanks to the miracle of movement and rest, and stretch my fingers and toes, sensing touch and precision, and my legs and arms, feeling strength and flexibility. You're doing the same now, testing these miraculous movements, and I marvel at what is to come.

To and fro we leap
And chase the frothy bubbles,
While the world is full of troubles
And is anxious in its sleep.

—William Butler Yeats

This week, I will:

- Be very open in my stillness, with my eyes closed and my hands on my belly, listening for you.

- Do at least one thing to maybe make our environment more peaceful. If I get upset, I'll breathe deeply and gently and focus only on my breath.

week 15

On clear quiet days,
when mind and body
are still,
I sense her presence
within me.

—Helen Whitaker

Flutterings! I am told that's what you will feel like. If I am still, I may perceive you. I shall lie here as motionless as I can, attentive only to the tiny flutterings inside. I have discovered that I like being still with you. In fact, in some ways, you have become my good little teacher.

I realize that often I move about too much. I'm busy, but

many of my doings are routine and habitual, with little purpose. Sometimes I go and go and go until I think I'll collapse. As I look at some of the trivial things that make me worry, or the many unimportant things I let take over my days, I realize I can choose to keep things simple and to focus on the stillness, learning from you that in this stillness is peace and contentment. By watching the sun, and how a plant will follow the sun, I realize that nature has a rhythm, just as you have a rhythm and I have a rhythm.

Today I'll watch the light. When light grandly moves to dark or when a cloud unveils the sun abruptly, my mood alters drastically. I wonder how my brash movements affect you. I'll do things evenly and with grace. I'll try to move like gradients of light bending throughout the day. Such a peaceful way to be: quiet and illuminated. I wonder if the great sun herself can penetrate my belly. Does she light your way? Do you glisten in delight and ride the bright amniotic waves?

At night, the mesmerizing moon shines through all the blackness. Sometimes she is round and large and full, much like my belly. Her light softly sighs through the night. When I introduce you to her spell, you'll be chirruping in delight, and all the nights of your life she will call to you.

I can allow the rhythms of nature to guide me. My movements will be even and graceful, and I'll accept what unfolds with calm.

"Come here" she said "I'll teach you a poem
I see the moon
The moon sees me
God bless the moon
And God bless me."

—Nikki Giovanni

This week, I will:

- Watch the light at least one day, paying attention throughout the day and evening.

- Honor my body's rhythms and rest when I am tired.

week 16

Beauty never slumbers;
All is in her name;
But the rose remembers
The dust from which it came.

— Edna St. Vincent Millay

Last month, you tripled in size; this month, you will only double. I hope that I don't mimic you. Getting used to my new body is difficult. I love the soft curves that you give me, yet sometimes I feel a bit anxious when I think about the changes as distortion rather than a swell of new life. Is it in this quiet month of being that your soul begins to form? Is there a place inside of you that remains apart, a place that reaches for the absolute, a place where you extend into infinity?

There is a place inside of me where my heart aligns with yours, a place that has nothing to do with our genes or my egg or your bloodline. It is an ancient place, where we meet in the darkness of all there is, a place where I unite with you in utter silence.

There will be many moments of speaking and touching and listening. Today, in the deep, restful quiet of my body, and in the imponderable formation of your soul, I rest at peace with you.

There is still a sacred hush about you. Your movements, like a distant rustle in a far-off bush, still elude me. I am content.

I enjoy the bond we share. You have helped to turn my focus from the outer world to a place much deeper and richer, a place I had forgotten for a while. I honor that inner place today.

Something austere hides, something uncertain
Beneath the deep bank calls and makes quiet music.

— Dylan Thomas

This week, I will:

- Slow my world to keep time with yours.

- Practice being fully present in the moment. When I am experiencing our connection, that is all I will do. I will do one thing at a time.

week 17

And sleep as I in childhood sweetly slept:
Untroubling and untroubled where I lie—
The grass below; above the vaulted sky.

—John Clare

Well, little cherub, this month seems to be about layers and coverings. My nails and hair are growing rapidly. I even have a visible line down my abdomen; *linea nigra* is its official name. I can no longer comfortably sprawl on my back in wild abandon. Soon it won't be good for our circulation. Left side, pillow between my knees, will be our sleep position. I'm feeling a bit restricted. Your presence is influencing every aspect of my being.

Your skin, delicate and translucent, is becoming thicker, hiding your blood vessels. I imagine your veins and their colorful rich lines like sea kelp, exquisite and just barely visible through a protective, sunbathed golden layer.

New cells are forming in the layers of your skin. One morning we'll collect the dew from the clover; close to the earth we'll bend. Later on we'll run by the sea and you'll feel the sand between your toes and the salty breeze on your flesh, and your skin wet from the water will greet the sun.

You waste nothing. Your dead skin cells are continually sloughing off and mixing with the oil from your skin glands. This great recipe becomes your *vernix caseosa*, a substance composed of downlike hair, scaly cells, and fatty gland secretions that gently coats your skin while you float in your amniotic fluid. How self-sufficient to manufacture your own little wet suit. Surf well in your watery world.

I trace the line on my abdomen with my finger, feeling the pressure of my skin and its flexible strength. I think of your skin growing strong and translucent, and then thickening, protecting your inner organs. I hope your skin is thick yet soft and pliable, wonderfully protective and ever so gently receptive.

I feel the warmth of air exhaled by coming Spring
As through my window screen I hear the insects sing.

—Liu Fang-Ping

This week, I will:

- Spend some time listening and feeling you, paying careful attention to your movements, your unique way of communicating with me.

- Seek a certain amount of expansion now other than in my belly. I'll keep up my regular daily exercise.

Daily exercise can be as easy as half an hour of movement such as stretching, walking, or rhythmic movements. This is great for you and the baby; he gets more oxygen and nutrients transported to him and you decrease fluid retention and facilitate his easy passage.

FIFTH MONTH

WEEK 18

Child, thou bringest to my heart
the babble of the wind and water,
the flower's speechless secrets, the cloud's dreams,
the mute gaze of wonder of the morning sky.

—Rabindranath Tagore

The skin on your palms and the soles of your feet is becoming thicker. With your bare hands and bare feet you can touch and explore and feel your world. Your life line is developing on your palm, reflecting the formation of your digestive and respiratory systems. I hope your life line will be long, deep, clean, and unbroken.

The middle line on your palm reflects the development of your nervous system. I wish you a strong and balanced constitution and a deep, intuitive awareness of yourself and others. Another palm line, the uppermost, is also developing, which reflects the development of your circulatory and excretory systems. May you let wisdom and joy flow through you, and may you excrete all that is evil and negative.

I hope that the lines of your palms and the major systems of your body that they represent coordinate smoothly, integrate easily, and reflect a genuine clarity and strength of being. According to Chinese medicine, your right palm reflects all my heritage. Your maternal grandmother, my mother, influences your digestive and respiratory line. I haven't the vaguest idea of what kind of eating binges she indulged in. Let's hope she liked grains and nuts and that she craved an occasional carrot for good luck. Your maternal grandfather, according to this tradition, influences your nervous system, and I hope he sent you peace and serenity.

I focus on your right palm and imagine the intricate development there and inside your body. I think of all the people who have come before you and how their genes are within you, yet you will thrive in your own way, and in your own time. With the choices I make now, I can do my best to help you thrive.

No need of motion or of strength,
Or even the breathing air:
I thought of Nature's loveliest scenes;
And with memory I was there.

—Dorothy Wordsworth

This week, I will:

- Think of the good things that I have received from my ancestors and let go of the rest.

- Enhance your nervous system by doing things to relax myself, perhaps a yoga video and my *Guided Meditation for a Healthy, Calm Pregnancy* CD that came with this book.

week 19

I am gone into the fields
To take what this sweet hour yields.
—Percy Bysshe Shelley

Let's consider your left palm. I'm grateful that it reflects your father's heritage. Sometimes I feel responsible for everything that comes along, and I'm pleased that this one palm shows that it isn't just you and me alone in this. When I feel overwhelmed, I remember that I'll do what I can but other things I can let go.

Your little hands are amazing; they tell so very much about you. May they reflect the constitutional strength I so desire for you. I can't wait to kiss each finger, each line. My wish for your palms is that they know love and healing and discretion.

You have been taking in proteins, fats, and minerals, and you are now discharging them in the form of fine hair. You are in balance. What an amazing little system you have. Spirals are developing on your skull, and the main one is at the crown of your head, to draw in the heavenly forces. May your body be filled with a divine energy, your own true self. You also have soft, fine hair on your back and arms and legs; you are gently furry. Your soft covering of hair is called lanugo. You'll probably shed this soft, downy covering during your first week after birth.

Now and then you're swallowing bits of your hair and a little of your *vernix caseosa*, all contained in your amniotic fluid. Some of this you can absorb through your digestive tract. It doesn't sound too palatable, but then again, neither do some of the foods I eat or that have been offered to me.

> From the lines on each of your palms, to the swirls of fuzzy hair on your head, to the tiny lines on your toes, I imagine each cell of your new body holds promise and receives love. I send them both to you and receive them in my own new and changing body.

He that question would anew
What fair Eden was of old,
Let him rightly study you,
And a brief of that behold.
Welcome, welcome, then . . .

—Robert Herrick

This week, I will:

- Eat one meal in silence, meditating on the taste, texture, and color of the food. I will eat slowly and chew many times before I swallow.

- Remain aware of my nutrition. I will also become aware of the environment in which I eat, always sitting quietly and never eating on the run.

week 20

No puddings just shouldings
No chocolate and goodings
Just raisins and kumquats
And spinach and green squash.

—Corinne Roussie

This is our halfway point. If you go to full term, you will be born forty weeks from day one of my last menstrual period. May your body, well dressed in an amniotic veil, continue to thrive.

I must continue to ensure that you get all the ingredients you need. It's difficult to drink eight glasses of water, eight ounces each, daily. That water is necessary to support the increased volume of blood in my body and to maintain your amniotic fluid. Freshly squeezed juice or milk is okay, too, but no soda, tea, coffee, or alcohol. Now and then, I find a cup of hot water soothing.

This halfway mark is reminding me of all I have to do. Sometimes I forget to exercise the muscle between my pubic bone in front and my tailbone (coccyx) in the back, sometimes called the Kegel muscle. If my Kegel is weak, it can't support your uterine home. If it's strong, it helps my bowel and bladder control.

> **Rest well beneath my heart chamber, little one. You have spent half your time within me, and you'll be in my arms when you've rested there just that much time again. I can be patient until that day arrives.**

The whole world is here on my body
Multiple coloralities bursting into spirit
Which is me.

—Ruth Lerner

This week, I will:

- Exercise my Kegel muscle.

- Continue to exercise daily, yet now I will choose less strenuous methods, such as prenatal yoga and walking or swimming.

Prenatal yoga classes are an excellent way to prepare for birthing, but *never* do any inverted poses (with feet above your head) during pregnancy.

Kegel muscle exercise: To tighten the Kegel muscle, squeeze the pelvic floor muscles as if you are preventing urination. Do this in sets of five at least ten times each day.

week 21

Like all vessels, fragile
Like all vessels too small
for the destiny poured into it.
—Rosario Castellanos

Some of what you take into your tiny body is indigestible, and your large intestine accumulates your waste in the form of a watery feces known as meconium. Such delicate waste, your meconium. The secretion of your bile into your intestinal tract causes it to take on a dark green color. All of this usually stays in your intestine until shortly after birth, when you discharge your uterine feedings. Will I get to change your first diaper?

By now you weigh practically two pounds. I'm a little ahead

of you in gaining weight. Right now, of course, I'm focusing on my nutrition and not on weight gain. Cheers to a bit of maternal fat.

My, how you are growing. The average length at this stage is thirteen inches long. That means you're a tad longer than a ruler. Do you ever stretch to your full length?

Even though it has been thickening, your skin is still thin, and you are so very fragile. I'm glad that you are well cushioned. I close my eyes and breathe a gentle caress across your flesh. I understand that your new skin is shiny, which makes me think it is pulled taut across your being. I wonder what you feel and whether you are comfortable in your commencement suit.

I think of your tiny form, and how your fingers and toes are printed as yours. You are developing your own fine definition. I pledge to guide you in placing your finger-prints with care and grace as you journey with your hands.

As a sweet organ harmony strikes the ear
So, for the primal mind, my eyes receive
A vision of your future drawing near.

—Dante Alighieri

This week, I will:

- Look around at all the varieties of noses and faces waiting in line at the bank or grocery store, and express gratitude for the differences and similarities that make us human.

- List the gifts my hands and feet have brought me, and think of how yours will serve you. As I walk, I'll think of my toes and how they help hold me erect and guide me, and my ankles and how they flex and bend yet hold me straight.

week 22

Here are threads, my true love, as fine as silk,
To knit thee, to knit thee,
A pair of stockings white as milk.

—Anonymous

Your eyelids are beginning to part. Take a peek at your surroundings and let your eyes be flooded by the rich fluid of your drift. Right now, you have barely any fat under your glistening skin. You do, however, have much protection and other kinds of coats and layers.

I don't know why, but when I think of you without any underlying fat, I want to protect you even more. I think I'll buy you a beautiful shawl today: warm, softly textured, and white.

You are sipping amniotic fluid daily. It's rather salty, as I recall. (It was once my liquid diet, too.) Let's drink to your health!

You have fluttering eyelashes now, all wet and beautiful, and eyebrows to go with them. You're becoming more and more complete day by day. There is certainly nothing routine about your days!

We couldn't be closer than we are now, and yet I long for the ability to caress you and cradle you in my arms. Somehow, close as you are, you feel a bit far away, as the constancy of my own heart does.

> As I close my eyes and feel my lashes brush my skin, I think of you and wonder what color your lashes will be, and how they will curl below your arching brows. I think of cradling you in my arms, wrapped in a snow-white shawl, and I smile with delight and joy.

Everyone suddenly burst out singing;
And I was filled with such delight.

—Siegfried Sassoon

This week, I will:

- Protect you by keeping your amnion strong when I eat well. I'll choose something dark green and leafy for lunch. Perhaps cooked spinach, chard, escarole, or bok choy, perhaps with a mound of tofu or cottage cheese for protein.

- Sip celery-and-beet juice. It's a great energizer!

- Listen to some joyous music.

A Perfectly Balanced Meal

1/2 cup almonds, or 1/4 cup sesame tahini or almond butter
1 cup cottage cheese, milk, or yogurt
1/2 cup brown rice, or 1/2 bagel
3/4 cup spinach, asparagus, kale, or mustard greens
3/4 cup yellow squash or carrots
1/2 cup cantaloupe or watermelon

SIXTH MONTH

WEEK 23

Let the dark walls that enclose you
tumble down!
Receive the lap of your mother the earth.
—Rosario Castellanos

Your lips are distinct this month. I'd love to see you grin from ear to ear! May your mouth be generous, loving, warm, and expressive. At this stage of your life, you are well proportioned, and I hope that continues into old age. I feel a bit out of proportion myself right now, so I'm glad one of us is in balance.

When I feel a bit out of balance or out of proportion, I meditate on the perfection of you. When I do this, my enthusiasm soars and I feel at one with your limitless potential.

Your eyes are developed, but your iris still lacks pigment. At birth, your eyes will be similar to those of the other "neonates" (that's what they'll call you at the hospital, you know). Their color will not be as sharp or clear as they will be when you are a bit older. With your eyes barely open, you experience the nature surrounding you. One day, we shall look at the stars together and laugh with the new moon.

You are growing and are enclosed in my womb, yet you know no limitations. I will balance fear of my own physical limitations with the knowledge that my limitations arise from your boundless potential and meditate on the perfection of you.

> *That then, is loveliness,*
> *we said,*
> *Children in wonder watching*
> *the stars,*
> *Is the aim at the end.*
> —Dylan Thomas

This week, I will:

- Send you my unbounded love and energy. I am here for you. You're so calm inside me. You bring me a deep sense of inner peace, and I send it back to you in loving reciprocity.

- Continue to eat foods rich in vitamins, especially vitamin A for your eyes. Perhaps I'll have a glass of carrot juice balanced with a handful of nuts for protein.

week 24

A measure of holiness a measure of power
A measure of fearfulness a measure of terror
A measure of trembling a measure of shaking
A measure of awe.

—Hebrew, third century A.D.

Sometimes I feel as though I need more support than I am receiving right now. I know this feeling is normal, but knowing that doesn't always help me feel better. Sometimes I feel very alone. No one can participate as I really want them to, because only I am carrying you. I wish your father would reassure me that he feels as deep a bond with you as I do. I need more physical involvement with your daddy, but some of my desires may be overwhelming to him right now.

Can I ever feel totally independent? I move from needing my mother to needing my husband. Now is not the time for distance. It is a time for forgiveness and closeness. I desire connection: physical, spiritual, and emotional.

I will honor my connection to you, my new child, and I will ask for the connection I need with others. I will surround you with love yet honor my own needs and desires.

To look at you gives joy;
your eyes are like honey,
Love flows over your gentle face.

—Sappho

This week, I will:

- Find a way to see some friends or spend time with my family, since social support is important to me right now.

- Ask my partner to cuddle for at least five minutes: no talking, just being happily together, caressing.

- Take a walk in the park with a friend or with my partner.

week 25

Heart to heart as we lay
In the dawning of the day.
—Robert Bridges

Your world is shifting now to one of sound. You can hear all the rumblings going on in your womb palace and even now and then outside voices. I try to stay calm and centered in hopes that my heart beats rhythmically and makes you feel safe.

The path between you and me is alive. You are the expansive bridge between mind and spirit. I hear the ring of your being inside me with great clarity. As you gestate within my womb, you make me know that all things are possible. You seem like the largo, or slow, movements of most baroque music. Surrounded by such beauty, our hearts beat restfully.

According to most studies, you and your unborn friends have a preference for Vivaldi, a baroque composer. Your fetal heart becomes steady, and your kicking declines when you listen to his music.

My heart calms with my breathing as I listen to soft music and align my breath into calmness. Like the soft rhythm of a cello, my breath is even and my heartbeat is soothing and sure.

Mingling me and thee,
When the light of eyes
Flashed through thee and me
Trust shall make us free
Liberty make wise.

—Algernon Charles Swinburne

This week, I will:

- Read aloud to you. I understand that you like repetition. I'll pick out a few books today and begin to read to you daily. Then, when you're born and I read to you, you'll remember and you'll be comforted.

- Find a comfortable place to rest and close my eyes. We will listen to Vivaldi, Handel, or another baroque composer.

week 26

O world invisible,
    we view thee,
O world intangible,
    we touch thee,
O world unknowable,
    we know thee,
Inapprehensible,
    we clutch thee!

—Francis Thompson

Now your brain is becoming mature enough that my behavior can be experienced by you emotionally. This is a new responsibility. Now I must deal with any ambivalence that I have about being a mother so I can send you all the warmth and love you deserve. Your daddy also has a big responsibility now. If his voice is any less than loving to me, you are annoyed by its sound but also you experience the result of my feelings. We both need to be surrounded by peaceful, loving, and supportive people.

I'll do my best to make certain that you know I love you. I'll continue to stroke my abdomen often because you like that.

You're now sending me messages by the way you kick and move about. Loud voices agitate you and even a bright light on my abdomen can stress you. If I sunbathe, I'll cover you gently. I'll demonstrate my love by heeding your gentle communications. Sometimes my emotions are so muted that I'm not quite aware of them. Our connection amazes me, and sometimes I wonder what you feel when I'm happy, or when I sing or hum or laugh.

Here we are sending messages back and forth to each other. The more I understand my own feelings, the more I can understand and respect yours. We're in this together, after all!

I can't be perfect. There will be times when I am upset and when certain events cause me stress. However, I make this commitment to you, little one: I shall not ignore you physically or psychologically on a consistent basis. I'll do the best I can to give you a healthy environment. Peaceful floatings.

We dance round in a ring and suppose,
But the secret sits in the middle and knows.

—Robert Frost

This week, I will:

- Listen to my dreams and work to understand them, thinking about them so that I understand how those messages and emotions affect you.

- Remember that silence is important. I'll be quiet and sit absolutely still for at least five minutes. I'll focus on my breath.

SEVENTH MONTH

WEEK 27

Sweet babe, in thy face
Soft desires I can trace,
Secret jobs and secret smiles,
Little pretty infant wiles.

—William Blake

We are repeating evolution, you and I. Since your conception, your nervous system and your brain have become increasingly complex. In this process you are repeating, and in you lie the origins of society. Our relationship affects all our attitudes toward life. Your arms, legs, eyes, ears, and blood vessels are partially a result of the environment we create together.

This channel filled with reassurance that we have flowing between us is another part of protecting you from all the uncertainties that you will encounter in your lifetime. The work we do in our silent time together is more important than all the politicians realize. Perhaps they could learn from us, from our bond.

I love that you reverberate like an endless hymn. My being hums with your being, and together we can make this world better, simply by our awareness and love, our combined humming.

In some sense, my brain regulates yours, and your brain regulates the functioning of your organs. I offer you social awareness and centered emotional responses, as you have offered me a connection to the universal cosmic consciousness.

A heart as soft, a heart as kind,
A heart as sound and free
As in the whole world thou canst find,
That heart I'll give to thee.

—Robert Herrick

This week, I will:

- Listen again to our baroque music and let go of all thoughts. Resting with my eyes closed, I let the music flood my being.

- Do something to bring peace to this planet, recognizing our oneness.

week 28

Deep, deep our love, too deep to show.
Deep, deep we drink, silent we grow.

—Du Mu

You reach and grasp with every bit of your being. I imagine and focus and push into what I think is infinite capacity, where at last I have grasped the endless—and then there you go again, taking boundless leaps.

We play together in the night. You kick and crawl in wondrous ceremony. Then you turn inside me. You magnetically draw me forward, then you leap and bound once more. I know that I shall silently meet you again today or tonight and that I shall feel you circulate and frolic in the splendor of your play. I shall feel you dance and swim and leap inside my womb. You are an endless stretch of wondrous breath, a rising hush of all there is. I delight in you.

You playfully flip and kick once more, making way for your independence. I look directly at you, and you kiss me softly with your knee.

I caress my belly and you float and rise in me. You whisper fathomless invitations, and I hear the echo of your form, sweet and ancient in the night. I relish our oneness and send you my joy to permeate every cell of your being.

Surely, I said
Now will the poets sing.
But they have raised no cry
I wonder why.

—Countee Cullen

This week, I will:

- Continue to eat and drink healthfully. I will recognize one unhealthy thought when it comes and transform it to a healthier belief.

- Contemplate all that I am consciously contributing to your growth and development. I shall be both accepting and willing to change what I can if it is important for our well-being.

WEEK 29

Give to these children new from the world,
Silence and love
And the long dew-dropping hours of the night,
And the stars above.

—William Butler Yeats

Well, our good nutrition is paying off. You are beginning to have some fat deposited under your skin, making you just a bit more cuddly. I'm growing rounder, too, of course. Sometimes, I wish I were eating chips and salsa, or maybe just chocolate, relaxing by the pool. Then I realize my choices today will help you grow, and I eat brown rice and steamed kale, perhaps spinach or lentil soup, and we both thrive. Your blood, cells, tissues, organs, and amniotic fluid are renewed by the foods I eat, after all.

When I feel fat and tired of being pregnant, I look forward to feeding you, to holding you in my arms and letting you suckle. I've seen pictures of babies in the womb, babies your age, sucking their thumbs. Have you found your thumb to suck, to comfort yourself? Soon you'll have other choices. My breasts are full and ready for you. Sometimes I feel you hiccup. Just because the volume of your amniotic fluid is diminishing doesn't mean you have to gulp it. Relax, little wonder. Soon you'll taste the sweet milk of my breast instead of the salty fluid of your amniotic ocean.

Right now, I feel full, full like a soft but firm pillow with all that is needed to nourish you: My heart swells with love as my belly swells with your growth and my breasts will swell with milk. I sense the fullness of this world I live in and the completeness of our love together.

Dear little saint of my life,
Deep in my breasts I feel
The warm milk come to birth.

—Federico García Lorca

This week, I will:

- Recall a time when I believed my intuition and followed it with good results, and I'll try to listen to my intuition. If I *know* something, with my strong inner *knowing*, I'll do my best to act on it, but I'll be careful to sort those things I fear, or worry about, from things I strongly "know."

- Practice letting go of at least one thing that is unnecessary to my well-being so that I can maintain my peace and happiness.

Dear little child of mine, I picture your hands and your mouth meeting in your watery world as you float and explore. I think of the changes in my own body as there to help you, and I massage my swollen belly with love. Most days, I choose healthy foods to feed you, and healthy thoughts to comfort you. We grow closer as we come nearer the time when I will rub your belly, and I will talk while seeing your face, and kiss you, yet we already talk, and my kisses are the thoughts I send you.

week 30

My heart is high above,
my body is full of bliss,
For I am set in luve as well
as I would wiss.

—Anonymous

Now you weigh about three pounds and you are about seventeen inches long. You still have a lot of growing to do, with only ten weeks left until your debut. I feel you kicking within me. Sometimes your movements are soft and gentle like the flutter of miniature angel wings, and I smile and touch you. Can you feel me? Other times, you seem rather playful and frisky; at other moments you seem to be trying to find the best and most comfortable position, squirming. I hope your umbilical cord doesn't get in your way.

I feel you again deep within me, and suddenly a wave of you ripples across the space. Like a barefoot gypsy beckoning the flamenco dancer from the cobblestone path to the soft-soled plains, you listen to the song I sing to you and roll and tumble quietly and rhythmically.

Sometimes, I picture how it will be when you are in my arms, not in my womb. I think of the night high in the vastness of the sky; the night soothes and rocks her midnight world. In a bassinet, wrapped in the soft cotton robes of a cloud, you are soothed in this veil of darkness and sleep, at peace.

> I feel you, and I am at times overwhelmed, and I feel unable and perhaps a bit unwilling to fathom you and me and our connection. Yet as I calm myself with my breathing, I know I can love you enough and nurture you enough.

Dance upon the shore;
What need have you of care
For wind or water's roar?
And tumble out your hair.

—William Butler Yeats

This week, I will:

- Choose a song that is ours. I'll sit peacefully with my hands on my belly and sing it to you. One day soon it will be one of your first memories.

- Relax more frequently, exercise more gently, and drink plenty of water.

week 31

And I am free to know
That you are bound to
> *me only by choice,*
> *that you are bound*
> *to me by love,*
And I am finally
Out of control.

—Helen Whitaker

You must stay in my womb for now. This is a crucial time and we must prevent the possibility of your being born prematurely. It's safe in there, I hope. I listen carefully for your subtle communications.

Amazing nuances of development are occurring. The muscles of your chest wall and diaphragm, enabling you to expand and contract during breathing, are being fine-tuned.

The reflex centers of your brain, which coordinate your muscles for breathing and for swallowing, are beginning to function. Again I'm reminded how important my diet is in providing the optimum development of your nervous system and the many dimensions of your body and mind. I try not to worry, since that is not healthy for either of us, but nutrition is so important, especially iron and vitamin B_{12} to prevent anemia.

You are well cushioned by your amniotic fluid, and I send my voice rippling across your waters. What name shall I call to you, child of mine? Whatever name we choose I shall sing to your ears and look on you, sweet child of mine, and try to allay all your fears.

This week, I will:

- Try pumpkin seeds, sesame seeds, and sunflower seeds. I'm doing my best to eat whole grains like millet and buckwheat, sea vegetables, and soybeans. I've learned that sea vegetables provide calcium and other nutrients, so I'm going to shop for hijiki, wakame, and arame, and though I don't always find the taste appealing, I can make a powder to sprinkle on soups, salads, and other foods.

- Sit quietly and say the names we're thinking of naming you aloud. Those names will be my meditation.

EIGHTH MONTH

WEEK 32

A fire-mist and a planet
A crystal and a cell,
A jelly fish and a saurian,
And caves where the
cave-men dwell;
Then a sense of law and beauty,
And a face turned from the clod;
Some call it evolution
And others call it God.

—William Herbert Carruta

I found out that you have a new trick. You can now turn your head from side to side. I just turned mine, realizing how amazing that must be when you do it for the first time. You're a bit more rounded this week, and I'm so happy you're still inside me. Please stay until you've reached term. It's a lot safer that way.

Your skin is now covered with white grease, your own little intrauterine outfit. I hope your worldly sense of fashion will be as natural and creative.

Right now, cotton seems to be my fashion statement. It's comfortable and allows my body energy to circulate freely. It keeps me warm or cool, whichever I need at the time.

For me, it's also important to massage my skin all over, especially my perineum and breasts. Sesame oil is so soothing, and ghee on my breasts will help prevent my nipples cracking. I'm preparing for you to stretch me vastly and for you to eat.

Everything I see vibrates within me and has the potential to nourish you. Every day until you're born will be a treasure hunt. We're both preparing for our new roles now, and as I await your debut I do what I can to prepare my body and my mind for the next phase of our life together.

Given conditions
As they be,
Desire no thing
Beyond what is
Now.

—Jack Crimmins

This week, I will:

- Acknowledge my yearning for harmony, peace, and serenity.

- Stroll one day with you in some beautiful spot, not waiting until you arrive "in person." It will be a mindful walk; I will be only in the moment, with no thoughts of past or future.

week 33

I'm on the shore and thou on the sea,
All of thy wanderings far and near,
Bring thee at last to shore and me.

—Bret Harte

After you arrive, you'll teach me many things. Each moment for you will be new, filled with all possibilities. Just contemplating you has enlightened me. Each moment for me is new also, but I don't often realize that. Thank you, baby guru.

I'm continuing to nourish us both. Frequent small meals are easier and more comfortable than three large ones. You take up a lot of space!

I know our prenatal vitamins, rich in iron and folic acid, are no substitute for food, but they are important as a supplement. I must remember to take them every day. I'm learning about continuity, order, routine, and responsibility—good lessons to learn before you are born.

Your daddy has a strong influence on my feelings and emotions. This is a time when we need to encourage and support each other more than usual. There is so much to talk about.

Our intimate connection is still intact. I have begun to think about the change in our relationship that will take place after you are born. There is a part of me that wants to hold you inside. I feel a bit anxious about severing our tie when you've reached term. I know it's important for you not to be forever attached to me. After all, this life you are now living inside of me is yours. I am here only to nurture and support you.

> At times, my realizations sometimes border on being overwhelming. When that happens, I breathe quietly and try to let go of expectation and worry, and simply feel. I feel my breath, my heartbeat, your gentle movements. I release worry and instead embrace love.

Come, for the soul is free!
In all the vast dreamland
There is no lock for thee,
Each door awaits thy hand.

—Bliss Corman

This week, I will:

- Discover how meditation is another important facet of simple vaginal birth, as is an acceptance of our impending new and different relationship.

- Begin to discuss parenting philosophy and practices with my partner.

week 34

The mulberry is a double tree.
Mulberry, shade me, shade me awhile,
It is a shape of life described
By another shape without a word
Mulberry, shade me, shade me awhile.

—Wallace Stevens

This week will be one of meditation. I will sit in a chair with my feet on the floor and my hands open in my lap. I'll close my eyes and focus on my exhalations for about five minutes. That's just the beginning. By the time you're born, we'll be seasoned meditators, you and I.

Another way I'll meditate is to sit for five minutes actively listening. I'll be listening to the silence of you within me, and you'll be listening to my heartbeat. A time of sitting perfectly still is such luxury. Peaceful floatings for you, peaceful sitting for me.

Meditation is good for my heart rate and my blood pressure. Even my digestion is affected positively. We're off to a deeper state of relaxation. This is a good way to prepare for labor, and it's a process where your participation is helpful.

When you are ready to be born, I want to be ready to open my cervix and my mind. I continue to take time to focus on my exhalations. I automatically inhale, as you will when you take your first breath. Now I'll practice alternating sending my exhalations down my right and left legs. Concentrating and focusing are important preparations for bringing you into the world.

Pregnancy, labor, and birth are natural. Women have been doing this for ages. I celebrate our silence in other ways of knowing, and the resonating harmony we share.

My mantra for labor will be: "All I have to do is keep my mind out of my body's way of the work it knows so well how to do." I will repeat this to myself now, relaxing and exhaling into the thought, letting it fill my mind and body, knowing that it is true.

And so in mountain
　　　Solitudes—o'ertaken as
　　　by some spell divine—
Their cares dropped from
　　　them like the needles shaken
From out the gusty pine.

　　　　　—Bret Harte

This week, I will:

- Observe my thoughts. I will not cling to them; I will not judge them; I will not push them away. I shall only observe them. It is a good way of letting go of what isn't necessary.

- Play my *Guided Meditation for a Healthy, Calm Pregnancy* CD.

week 35

At times a fragrant breeze comes floating by,
And brings, you know not why,
A feeling as when eager crowds await
Before a palace gate.

—Henry Timrod

Since I don't want anything to interrupt the course of your vital flow, I think it's important to be aware of the seven energy centers in our bodies. One is at the base of my spine (and yours, too, of course), and one is below my navel; that one is important during labor. I'll focus on these two places now, while sending my breath to free the energy that might need unhinging with focused breathing. I'm getting better at this. It may seem strange, but it's actually rather fun.

A third energy center is right around my navel; if it is blocked, it can interfere with my digestion. Energy center number four is right in the center of my chest, between my two nipples; this is the heart center, and from it flows love to you. The fifth is in my throat and has to do with communication and creativity. You and I are doing pretty well in that area, I think. Just to make sure these three areas are functioning as well as possible, I'll focus my exhalations on them. No kicking for a moment or two, please.

The sixth energy center is located between my eyebrows (something you recently grew). This is the area on which yogis focus when they walk on fire so they feel no pain. I wonder how painful contractions are. On a scale of one to ten, I think they're a ten or maybe even off the scale. If the yogis can do it, I can at least imagine being able to attain a pain scale of three. Now, I will focus on the point between my eyebrows and imagine an easy, pain-free birth.

Energy center number seven is located at the top of my head. I think about your magical head and how your bone plates slide together to safely reduce the diameter of your skull as you pass through me on your way out and into my arms. The thought of your descent at once thrills me and makes me a bit anxious. I hope there is room for you as you wend your way through the birth canal. I worry about it sometimes. Now I send my breath to protect your crowning soft spot. Your body is so flexible. May your spirit be the same.

Could it be true that you are wiggling your way downward? I feel a bit more room in my upper abdomen and I can breathe freely again. My lungs are expanding with great joy at each inhalation. I had forgotten how pleasurable a long, deep inhalation can be. I look forward to your first breath and hope it will be as wondrous to you as it will be to me.

Still there's a sense of
blossoms yet unborn
In the sweet airs of morn.

—Henry Timrod

This week, I will:

- Read about the energy centers and focus where indicated for a few moments at a time.

- Continue my peaceful birth preparation by listening to my *Guided Meditation for a Healthy, Calm Pregnancy* CD.

NINTH MONTH

WEEK 36

I never saw a moon,
I never saw the sea;
Yet know I how the heather looks,
And what a wave must be.

—Emily Dickinson

What is it like to breathe for the first time? Is it like inhaling the first scent of spring that arrives on a gentle breeze, or is it like a thrust of a cold winter's gale, harsh and penetrating upon your entire being?

Oh, you are so safe, so protected! I don't care that you are now perched in such a fashion that there is more pressure on my bladder and my rectum. I am getting tired of being pregnant, and yet the thought of you floating inside of me is more soothing than considering your sliding forth into this vast world. It's difficult for me to feel comfortable at all now. Lying on my left side gives some relief. What about you? Can you feel my mounting excitement? Do you know it's getting close to your arrival? Are you ready? Actually, this is a delightful place. You won't be cramped anymore, yet you'll feel safe. I'll protect you.

Very soon you'll be making a journey all by yourself into this world, through the birth canal. As I breathe quietly now, I think that will be a joyous ride, if scary, but we'll both be filled with love and wonder at the end, and that will be only the beginning of the life we'll share. Rest for the journey, little one.

I think a lot about my participation in your outbound journey. I promise to make it as short and easy as possible. To prepare, I'm listening to my *Guided Meditation for a Healthy, Calm Pregnancy* CD. I'm taking my birthing classes and learning to relax my jaw and my hands as I visualize sending my breath all the way through my body and out through my vagina.

Hug me round
In your solitude
Profound.
—Georgia Douglas Johnson

This week, I will:

- Give you my undivided attention for twenty minutes daily from now on. We shall meditate together and visualize your passage.

- Use my breathing to practice focusing as I'll do during labor. I will also pick out the music I'll use in the birthing room.

Repeat this simple meditation aloud to yourself, using the "so hum" phrase to stretch out your breath and make it vibrate through your body, relaxing and releasing tension. *So.* I breathe in the healing forces of the universe and, *hum,* I exhale my ego-bound limitations. *So hum. So hum. So hum. So hum. So hum. So hum.*

week 37

High between dream and
day and think how there
The soul might rise visible
as a flower.

—E. J. Scovell

My body, in its great archetypal wisdom, knows exactly how to give birth to you just as the earth knows how to give blossom to the flowers.

Sometimes I wonder if I can birth you vaginally. I really don't want a C-section. I close my eyes, and I visualize you and me at term. I have a lot of tension in my body when I think of birthing you. I increase the tension in my feet, legs, chest, arms, and hands; then I release it. I inhale through my nose and breathe in the healing forces from the universe as my abdomen rises with my breath. I then slowly release my breath through my mouth, sending it deep into my perineum. I focus on the peacefulness of you within me.

I sit here quieting my anxious mind by focusing on my breath. As I breathe in and breathe out, as I focus on each inhalation and exhalation, I am almost in a trance. This week, you receive your own breath. Your lungs mature, which means that when you are born your respirations will be as easy and as natural as mine are now. I imagine you here, fresh and new and wet on my abdomen, your breath and my breath rising and falling in unison. One day, we'll go to the headlands high above the ocean; the seagulls will soar and ride the wind while you and I fill our lungs with the clear air. We'll laugh and shout with glee as we breathe without a thought and look together at the colors of the wildflowers and the sky. Develop, little lungs, make yourselves complete! It's not long before your first respiration.

Each day I think gratefully of how our bodies, yours and mine, know what to do. Our wisdom comes from a greater wisdom, and as the seagulls know how to swoop and soar, we also know how to be. I sit as comfortably as I can in a chair with my feet flat on the floor. I focus on the perfection of you, and I send a healing white light from the center of my two brows to the center of yours. A brilliant white umbilicus of light flowing from me to you and from you to me.

Mother and child,
　　lover and lover mated,
Are wound and bound
　　together and enflowing
What has been plaited
　　cannot be unplaited.

—May Sarton

This week, I will:

- Close my eyes and relax my jaw whenever I remember to. I will practice sending every other inhalation deep into my uterus and out through my cervix and my vagina.

- Prepare with gentle stretches, gentle thoughts, plenty of water, and rest, and listen to my meditation CD.

Dear Baby: if you stay within a bit longer, I will rest peacefully so that you can reap more of the benefits from your uterine hideaway. Gather all the immunities you can; eat and drink of me, supping to your heart's delight. My body is still your home for now. I have done my best for it so I can carry you to term. Love, Mommy.

week 38

Let love embrace the ten thousand things;
Heaven and earth are a simple body.

—Hai Shih

My abdomen is grand with the size of you. I want you to stay, yet I'm feeling uncomfortable. Now for a moment I rest in silence. I send my thoughts out to sea. I let go of my fear and tension. I breathe in the serenity of a vast blue sky, and I send that calm throughout my body. I float on the fluffy cumulus clouds, and my body feels free and weightless. I am at peace as we journey together, abandoning ourselves in silence.

I've heard that formula is easier than breast-feeding. I still have some reservations about the process of nursing you. The way I see it, my milk is ready to flow for you. It would be a shame to deprive you of that wonderful bond that we can continue to develop. Its temperature is perfect for you. It has all the nutrients you need. You are less likely to get sick if I suckle you. When I think of all the chores of life I must deal with after you are born, I can't think of any more delightful respite than to sit with you as a life force from my breast trickles into your eager mouth.

Again I contemplate relaxing and feeding you. I shall make the time to nurse you for at least three to six months. It's also good for my uterus. Nursing you reduces the risk of hemorrhage and causes my uterus to return to its normal size quickly and naturally. That's certainly a plus. It also helps me get back in shape.

If I breast-feed you, you will have a much smaller chance of having upper respiratory infections, ear infections, and colon infections. You'll be less likely to have allergies, and you'll be calmer. All of this also means that I'll have more time to do what I need and want to do. If I feel anxious or uncomfortable or feel as though I don't know what I'm doing, I'll ask for help.

When you arrive, I'll massage you with sesame oil. Until

then, I'll pay special attention to you through my enormous belly. Every time I touch my abdomen, you seem to answer with a gesture: your first game.

As your debut approaches, I remind myself that when I stay in the present moment, in the now, I feel safe. I can trust my relaxed body, and I can trust you to find your way into this world from your peaceful floatings.

Sing when you're happy
and from worries keep away!

—Luo Yin

This week, I will:

- Practice this labor meditation: You are still growing, and I'm curious how you will manage to squeeze through your birthing passage. I send to you a white light of love and lubrication. I imagine you, at term, being guided down through my body on this path of light, surrounded by it and filled with it. The same light softens, ripens, and easily dilates my cervix and pushes you out into the baby catcher's hands. It is with great ease that we perform this miracle.

- Take a warm bath before sleep, a practice first-stage-of-labor bath. I'll add two to three drops of rose water to the water, then I'll relax, soak, empty my mind, and focus on the rise and fall of my abdomen for ten minutes. I'll climb into bed totally relaxed and I'll sleep peacefully.

Rose water can be purchased in the baking aisle of most grocery stores and is better than scented oils for labor.

WEEK 39

*Days and months appear
long in the fairyland halls.*

—Bai Ju-Yi

I plan to relax with you daily this week. Soon our labor will begin. I know whatever I think and feel and hear affects you. I know whatever drugs I take during labor will also affect you. I'll do my best to give you a drug-free beginning. I want to have an alternative to drugs.

I wonder if you somehow sense that you will soon be moving from your warm and dark fluid habitat to a very bright and spacious world. I'm feeling all sorts of different physical sensations, which I'm certain you must be experiencing also. You don't have very much space in there anymore. I feel excited, a little impatient, and somewhat uncertain.

> Now that the time is near, I visualize myself strong and physically ready for the transition from prenatal mothering to accepting you into my arms and life and knowing that my strength will rise to meet the challenges. Just as my mind-body has let you grow and thrive within, so my mind-body will help you grow and thrive in life, and we'll learn together, you and I, seeking and finding help when we need it.

Ah! When will this long
weary day have end,
And lende me leave to come unto my love?
How slowly do the houres
theyr numbers spend!
—Edmund Spenser

THE INVITATION

Dear Baby: Today I send you an invitation. You have been a most welcome resident, although I hope that you don't stay inside for too much longer. Outside, the sun shines, the flowers bloom and toss scents of pleasure in the air, the clouds play tag, and the butterflies do the same. Rain falls and rivers flow, trees grow high in the sky, vegetables grow from the earth; gentle breezes will kiss your face, and stems of nipples with streams of milk are waiting for your wanting mouth. Last, but not least, I cannot possibly grow another inch. Do come soon. Love, Mommy.

The rising sun appears
sublime
But O! 'Tis near your
birthing time.

—Anonymous

This week, I will:

- Prepare us nutritionally for this labor. I need to eat several small meals a day, as there seems to be very little room for anything more. Oatmeal, cottage cheese, nuts, seeds, soy milk, warm miso soup, vegetables, egg whites, and some apples—simple, nourishing, and fresh, similar to a marathon runner's diet.

- Soak again in a warm bath with some lavender if my bag of waters has not yet broken when the first stage of labor arrives. This will help my uterus contract more efficiently and will reduce the pressure I feel from inside of me.

WEEK 40

Last night, I pulled the
moon down
out of the sky and onto my
waiting belly.

—Ruth Lerner

We are a team, you and I, a unique collaborative system. Let me explain how it will work, and how our bodies will work together. There are molecules that regulate the production of progesterone in your fetal membranes, in my placenta, in the lining of my uterus, and in the muscle cells of my uterus. When the prostaglandin-regulating molecules inhibit the progesterone production, the process of birth begins. As the time approaches, I visualize the progesterone decreasing and the prostaglandin increasing.

I visualize the molecules as friendly and competent. They aid my cervix in softening and dilating. Let the process of birth begin! I hope that my pituitary gland soon secretes oxytocin, a hormone that is another factor in the contracting of my uterus. I visualize all of the secretions effectively causing the muscles of the wall around you, my uterine wall, to contract. This gentle momentum is how birthing begins and proceeds until you and your placenta have arrived.

> Come, my wonderful child, let my uterus usher you down the birth canal! I realize that you begin the process of birth and that I must be ready in order to complete it. I am ready. I await you.

So waste not thou; but come for all the vales
Await thee; azure pillows of the hearth
Arise to thee; the children call, and I
Thy shepherd pipe, and sweet is every sound
Sweeter thy voice, but every sound is sweet;
Myriads of rivulets hurrying thro' the lawn,
The moan of doves in immemorial elms
And murmuring of innumerable bees.

—Alfred, Lord Tennyson

This week, I will:

- Not sit and wait for you. I'll go to the garden or to the park. I'll walk and admire other creations. I'll listen to music and do anything I can to keep my mind out of my body's way.

- Imagine my contractions as coordinated and efficient. Enjoy the full massage as your head and body easily move through the gentle stimulation of your first passage.

Moon of the Ninth Month
Cast its shadow.
How weary is the life within
When it sees its dark prison
It struggles to be free
And make its camp on earth.

—Native American birthing song

THINGS TO TAKE TO THE BIRTHING room

- Cotton clothes to wear

- Cotton socks

- CD player

- Gregorian chant or baroque music CD

- Warm miso soup in a thermos to sip during labor

- Rolling pin in case of back labor

- Rose water

- Something beautiful to look at, perhaps a photo from a magazine

- Bubbles for blowing to enhance relaxation during labor

- Phone number for the local La Leche League for breast-feeding support

- A support person, either family, friend, or professional

- Birthing ball (if not already available in the birthing room)

OTHER RESOURCES BY
MICHELLE LECLAIRE O'NEILL

*Hypnobirthing Bundle for Happy Hypnomoms
and Blissful Hypnobabies*

Creative Childbirth

CD 1: *Hypnosis for Pregnancy*

CD 2: *Hypnosis for Labor*

CD 3: *Music for Pregnancy, Labor, and Breast-Feeding*

Hypnobirthing: The Leclaire Method

Twelve Weeks to Fertility

Meditation and Healing CD

Healing from Stress and Trauma (Six CDs)

Michelle Leclaire O'Neill, Ph.D., R.N.,
is available for consultation by telephone.

For details visit www.leclairemethod.com or call 310-454-0920.

ABOUT THE AUTHOR

Michelle Leclaire O'Neill, Ph.D., R.N., has worked in the field of psycho-neuroimmunology for the past sixteen years. She was on the staff of the Simonton Cancer Center in southern California for ten years. While there, she taught meditation, imagery, their two-year health plan, dealing with death and dying as part of life, and getting well again. As a balance to her work with cancer patients, Dr. O'Neill began working with reproductive health and preventive medicine.

She developed the Leclaire Childbirth Method, the first childbirth method developed by a woman; coined the word *hypnobirthing* and created the Hypnobirthing Method; and created the Mind Body Fertility Program, which she teaches at various locales and expects to write about in her next book. She lectures and speaks extensively on her program. She counsels and works from her Mind Body Center in Pacific Palisades, California. She is the mother of three children. Her Web site is www.leclairemethod.com.